Christmas

Make Everyone Smile in Christmas with Jokes

Copyright © 2022

All rights reserved.

DEDICATION

The author and publisher have provided this e-book to you for your personal use only. You may not make this e-book publicly available in any way. Copyright infringement is against the law. If you believe the copy of this e-book you are reading infringes on the author's copyright, please notify the publisher at: https://us.macmillan.com/piracy

# Contents

Adult Christmas Jokes 1
Dirty Christmas Jokes 11
Funny Holiday Jokes Ideas 24

Adult Christmas Jokes

It's never too early to spread some Christmas cheer, and even if you're not a huge fan of the holidays, here is something that'll make this year's season a little lighter.

Whether you can't wait to share Christmas humor with your friends or are drunk from Christmas dinner and want some dirty holiday jokes or Santa jokes for adults to pass around the table, we've got you covered with these 29 jokes that are pretty much PG-13.

Keep reading!

Santa jokes for adults

1) Q: What do you call a kid who doesn't believe in Santa?

A: A rebel without a Claus.

2) Q: Why is Santa so jolly?

A: Because he knows where all the naughty girls live.

3) Q: Why is Christmas just like your job?

A: You do all the work and the fat guy with the suit gets the credit.

4) Q: What do you call a broke Santa?

A: Saint Nickel-less

5) Q: Why did Santa send his daughter to college?

A: To keep her off the North Pole.

6) Q: What do you call Santa if he also lives in the South Pole?

A: Bi-Polar.

7) Q: What did Santa sing when he went down the chimney?

A: "Chestnuts roasting on an open fire..."

8) The Santa at the shopping mall was quite surprised when he saw Martha, a woman in her mid-twenties, asking to sit on his lap. We all know Santa doesn't usually take requests from adults, but she smiled at him very nicely and he ended up asking her what she wanted for Christmas.

"Something for my mother, please," she replied. "Something for your mother? That's very loving and thoughtful of you," smiled Santa. "What would you like me to bring her? Emily answered quickly, "A son-in-law."

9) Q: What nationality is Santa Claus?

A: North Polish.

10) Q: Why does Santa Claus go down the chimney on Christmas Eve?
A: Because it soots him.

11) Q: What do you call Santa's helpers?

A: Subordinate clauses.

12) Q: What's the difference between Santa and a knight?
A: One slays the dragon, the other drags the sleigh.

13) Q: What did Santa say to his wife?

A: It's going to reindeer.

14) Q: What goes "oh oh oh"?

A: Santa walking backwards.

15) Q: What do you call people who are afraid of Santa Claus?
A: Claustrophobic.

Christmas jokes for adults

15) Q: Why are Christmas trees so fond of the past?

A: Because the present's beneath them.

16) Q: Why did the snowman want a divorce?

A: Because his wife was a total flake.

17) Q: What do you call an elf who sings?

A: A wrapper!

18) Q: What's the difference between the Christmas alphabet and the ordinary alphabet?

A: The Christmas alphabet has Noel.

19) Q: Why did the Grinch rob the liquor store?

A: He desperately needed some holiday spirit.

20) Q: What do priests and Christmas trees have in common?

A: Their balls are ornamental.

21) Wanna see the North Pole? ... At least that's what Mrs. Claus calls it.

22) Q: How do snowmen make babies?

A: Snowballs, of course.

23) Q: What do the female reindeer do when the guys are out working?
A: They go into town and blow a few bucks.

Dirty Christmas jokes

24) Q: Why doesn't Santa have any kids?

A: Because he only comes once a year.

25) Q: What's Santa's safe sex tip?

A: Wrap your package before shoving it down the chimney.

26) Q: Why does Santa land on the roof?

A: Because he likes it on top.

27) If your left leg is Thanksgiving and your right leg is Christmas, do you mind if I visit between the holidays?

28) Q: What do a train set and boobs have in common?

A: They were both made for kids but dads can't help playing with them.

29) Three men died on Christmas Eve and were met by Saint Peter at the gates of heaven. "In honor of this holy season," he said, "You must each possess something that symbolizes Christmas to get into heaven."

The first man fumbled through his pockets and pulled out a lighter. He flicked it on. "This represents a candle," he said.

"Very well, you may pass through the pearly gates," said Saint Peter.

The second man reached into his pockets and pulled out a set of keys. They jingled as he shook them and he said, "They're bells."

Saint Peter said, "You may also enter heaven."

The third man started searching desperately through his pockets and finally pulled out a pair of women's panties. Saint Peter looked at the man, puzzled. "And just what do those symbolize?" he asked with a raised eyebrow.

The man replied, "These are Carol's."

Merry Christmas, you guys. If you're on the naughty list, we hope these jokes filled you with some cheer.

Dirty Christmas Jokes

Naughty List or Nice List? Who cares! We're all adults now and ready to cut loose and have a little fun for the remainder of the year. We want to read literotica, send those scandalous sexts, use those Christmas pick up lines, and instigate some dirty truth or dare fun with our baes and friends. First, though, we want to tell some truly bad and extra dirty jokes about Christmas.

Before we do, though, suffice it to say that some of what you're about to read may turn your cheeks redder than Rudolph's nose. Blush away! When it's cold outside, no one knows the difference between a face flush from feelings and a face flush from the frigid air. It's really the best time of year to indulge in a little naughty fun if you think about it that way.

Of course, there are things that live in the dark corners of the internet that could land you on Santa's naughty list for life. So, you may not want to go poking around too much. Luckily, we've gone ahead and rounded up some NSFW, adults-only jokes that'll have you spit-laughing out that eggnog come the holidays. So relax, unwind, and, enjoy these funnies responsibly.

1. What do snowmen use to make snowbabies?

Snowballs.

2. What do a train set and your wife's breasts have in common?
They were both made for kids but you can't help playing with them.

3. How does Santa practice safe sex?

He always wraps his package before shoving it down the chimney.

4. What do three hos get you?

One very jolly Santa.

5. Why does Santa always come through the chimney?

Because he knows better than to try the back door.

6. How is Christmas just like any other day at the office?

You do a bunch of work and some guy in a suit gets all the credit.

7. Why do elves laugh when they run?

Because the snow tickles their balls.

8. Why doesn't Santa have kids of his own?

He only comes once a year.

9. What does The Grinch do with a baseball bat?

Hits a gnome and runs.

10. What do you get if you deep-fry Santa Claus?

Crisp Cringle.

11. What's the most disappointing thing for a lover on Christmas morning?

When they get a sweater, but they're hoping for a screamer or a moaner.

12. Why did the Snowman want a divorce?

Because his wife was a total flake.

13. Why did the Grinch hit up the liquor store?

He was desperate for some holiday spirit.

14. One Christmas, a little boy wrote to Santa Claus saying, "Please send me a sister."

Santa Claus wrote him back, "Okay, please send me your mother."

15. What did Santa sing when he went down the chimney?

"Chestnuts roasting on an open fire…"

16. What do you call an elf wearing earmuffs?

Whatever the hell you want. He can't hear you.

17. I love this time of year.

You can slam your laptop shut when your partner walks into the room and you don't get any disgusted looks.

18. Say your left leg is Thanksgiving, and your right leg is Christmas…

Can I visit between the holidays?

19. Why does Mrs. Claus always pray for a white Christmas?

Cause she's married to a guy who comes once a year.

20. What do you call people who are afraid of Santa Claus?
Claustrophobic.

21. As I was paying the cashier for my Christmas tree, he asked,

"Are you going to put that up yourself?"

I said, "No, I'm putting it up in the living room."

22. Why are Christmas trees better than men?

Even the small ones give satisfaction.

23. Why does Santa always land on your roof?

Because he likes it on top.

24. Why is Santa so damn jolly?

Because he knows where all the naughty women live.

25. Why was the snowman smiling?

He could see the snowblower coming down the street.

26. Why did Santa divorce Mrs. Claus?

He was obsessed with getting the cookie.

27. You know, that's not a candy cane in my pocket…

I'm just THAT happy to see you.

28. Is your name Jingle Bells?

Cause you look ready to go all the way.

29. Are you Christmas? 'Cause I wanna merry you!

Are you Hall? Cause I wanna deck the Hall.

30. What's the difference between snowmen and snowwomen?
Snowballs.

31. Wanna see the North Pole?

That's what Mrs. Claus calls it…

32. What do you call Santa's helpers?

Subordinate clauses.

33. What does Mrs. Claus get when she wears tight pants?

A Mistletoe.

34. Why does Santa always have a full sack?

Because he only comes once a year!

35. What do all the female reindeer do when Santa takes the males out to guide his sleigh?

They go into town and blow more than a few bucks.

36. What's the difference between Tiger Woods and Santa?

Santa was smart enough to stop at three hos.

37. Dear Santa…

Define good.

38. Little boy: Dear Santa, please send me a baby brother

Santa: Send me your mother

39. Santa saw your Instagram photos. You're getting clothes and a dictionary for Christmas.

40. Dear Santa, I would like a new birth suit this year. The old

one is wrinkly and sagging. Thank you!

41. What do you call a kid who doesn't believe in Santa?

A rebel without a Claus.

42. What does One Direction and my Christmas tree have in common?

They both have ornamental balls.

43. Why did Santa send his daughter to college?

To keep her off the North Pole.

44. What's the difference between a Christmas tree and Santa?

A Christmas tree will stay up for 12 nights, has cute balls, and looks good with the lights on.

45. Why does Santa Claus like to get naughty after coming down the chimney?

Because it soots him.

46. What happened when Mr. and Mrs. Claus got randy beneath the Christmas tree?

She came down with tinselitis!

47. Why was the elf having trouble with his libido?

He had low elf-esteem.

48. Why is Santa so jolly?

Because he knows where all the naughty girls live.

49. What did Santa sing when he went down the chimney?

Chestnuts roasting on an open fire…

50. The Santa at the shopping mall was quite surprised when he saw Martha, a woman in her mid-twenties, asking to sit on his lap. We all know Santa doesn't usually take requests from adults, but she smiled at him very nicely and he ended up asking her what she wanted for Christmas.

"Something for my mother, please," she replied.

"Something for your mother? That's very loving and thoughtful of you," smiled Santa. "What would you like me to bring her?"

Emily answered quickly, "A son-in-law."

Funny Holiday Jokes Ideas

'Tis the season to snicker! These holiday jokes celebrate the funny side of the festive season.

Just Desserts

Q: Did you hear about the man who stole an Advent Calendar?
A: He got 25 days.

Choose Your Own Spelling

Me: [Searches 'Chanukah']

Google: Did you mean Hanukkah?

Me: I DON'T KNOW, GOOGLE. NO ONE DOES

Hip Hop Holiday

Q: What kind of Christmas music do elves like?
A: Wrap music!

The Most Punderful Time of the Year

You: I love this time of year!

Me: You mean you 'ove' it.

You: What?

Me: Because there's Noël. —**@tiemoose**

Polar Opposites

People act like the North Pole and the South Pole are exactly the same, but really, there's a whole world of difference between them.

For more grins (and groans), check out this collection of our favourite dad jokes.

Avian Obsession

"The Twelve Days of Christmas" is completely unrealistic. There is no way that you're still accepting gifts from someone after four days of birds.

Famous Last Words

"Let's go get a Christmas tree!" — A divorce story.

Achievable Goals

I bought a treadmill because my New Year's resolution is to have more things to put my laundry on.

Holiday Hit

"All that time spent selecting and decorating, and a week after [Christmas], you see the tree by the side of the road, like a mob hit. A car slows down, a door opens, and a tree rolls out." —Jerry Seinfeld

Frosty Gets Fit

Q: What do you call a snowman with a six pack?

A: An abdominal snowman.

Feline Friends

I don't know who's worse, the people who sign their cats' names on Christmas cards or the cats who refuse to sign.

World's Worst Office Parties

The Tonight Show Starring Jimmy Fallon asked people to submit their worst Christmas office party stories. Here's what people sent in:

– I stayed sober to avoid embarrassing myself in front of my coworkers. Then my heel broke, and I fell into the punch bowl.

– My boss ordered two pizzas for 15 employees, then ate one all by herself.

– My coworker got so drunk, he asked his girlfriend whether she was single. She said yes.

– I did a Secret Santa gift exchange; mine got me a can of creamed corn.

Two in One

My kids: Can we decorate for Christmas now?!

Me: Sure. [Puts Santa hat on pumpkin.]

Fa-la-la-la-la

Q: What did the peanut butter say to the grape on Christmas?

A: 'Tis the season to be jelly!

Fast Wrapper

My wife: How many presents did you get wrapped?

Me [proudly]: Four.

Wife: In an hour?

Me: They were oddly shaped

Peace and Quiet

Q: What's a parent's favourite Christmas carol?

A: Silent night!

One Step at a Time

I like to put up Christmas decorations in stages. This is the stage where I sit on the couch with lasagna and stare at the boxes.

Create Your Own Carol

How to make a Christmas song:

Add sleigh bells

That's it, you're done

Can you guess the oldest Christmas carol? (Hint: It's not Silent Night!)

Mistaken Identity

Our new neighbours thought our Wi-Fi network was our last name. So when they gave us a Christmas card, they addressed it to "The Linksys Family." —via HuffingtonPost.com

Starting Strong

My New Year's resolution is to be more assertive, if that's ok with you guys?

Bad Behaviour

Q: Which of Santa's reindeer has the worst manners?

A: Rude-olph!

Bought or Borrowed

To all those who received a book from me as a Christmas present…they're due back at the library tomorrow.

Academy Award Winner

My performance in "I'm so sad I can't make it to your Christmas party" is already generating Oscar buzz.

The First Noel

Q: What did Adam say the day before Christmas?

A: It's Christmas, Eve!

Why Stop at 12?

On the 13th day of Christmas, my true love said to me, "I think I might be a hoarder."

Christmas with the Crown

Prince Philip looks out the window on Christmas Eve. "That's some reindeer," he says.

The queen replies, "65 years. Yes, that is a lot." —Via express.co.uk

Forged Signature

For the longest time, I thought my mother, father, and cat all had the same handwriting. Then I found out Mom was just signing cards for all of them. —Michelle Wolf, comedian

Find out what the holidays looked like 100 years ago.

Sweet Dreams

Q: What does the Gingerbread Man use to make his bed?
A: Cookie sheets!

Putting a Face to the Names

The office holiday party is a great place to meet everyone you've been emailing from ten feet away. —@**someecards**

If you got a kick out of that one, you'll love these **funny work cartoons**.

Selling Out

Jeez, did Santa's agent turn down a single commercial? —**Jim Gaffigan**, comedian

These **Christmas brain teasers** will give your grey matter a workout.

Second Chances

For those of you who have already failed your New Year's resolution, like I have, there is always the Chinese New Year to try again. — @ThomasPankonin

Check out these **Chinese New Year traditions** we can all celebrate.

Seasonal Syntax

Q: What do you call Santa's helpers?

A: Subordinate Clauses.

Ready to put your vocabulary to the test? See if you can match these **Christmas words** with their proper definitions.

Comfort Food

I understand now why Hanukkah happens when it does. We could all use a little light right now. And fried stuff. —Jess Zimmerman, editor

Read about one family's **annual Hanukkah tradition,** complete with latkes and lakes.

Baa Humbug

Q: What's a sheep's favourite Christmas song?

A: Fleece Navidad.

Literally Christmas

It was the beginning of December. I noticed my four-year-old putting on her hat and coat, so I asked her where she was going. She said she wanted to see if Christmas was really just around the corner. —Lynn Krochak

Check out these **funny tweets every parent can relate to**.

Time for a Rewrite?

Think how much more exciting "Dreidel, Dreidel, Dreidel" would be if they'd written it after the dreidel was dry and ready. — @Mikelffingwell

Find out **why Hanukkah changes dates each year**.

Gone to the Dogs

My mom is angry with me for letting the dogs see their presents before tomorrow morning. Apparently, I ruined their Christmas. — @akfarizel

Going for Broke

Q: What do you call a bankrupt Santa?

A: Saint Nickel-less.

Equal parts heartbreaking and hilarious, we asked 20 people to reveal **how they learned the truth about Santa Claus.**

Santa on the Brain

Christmas: the time when everyone gets Santamental.

The Ultimate Gift

One of my four nephews just brought me wine and said, "Here's your Christmas juice," and now he's the one I'm leaving everything to. — **@Kendragarden**

Check out these uniquely **Canadian holiday traditions**.

Chimney Sweep

Q: What's red and white and falls down chimneys?

A: Santa Klutz.

Christmas Wish

The older you get, the more holidays become about keeping your father off a ladder. —@**shutupmikeginn**

Make sure to avoid these common **holiday safety mistakes**.

Made in the USA
Monee, IL
12 December 2022